The Death Of A Matriarch
The Death Of My Family

THE DEATH OF A MATRIARCH
– The Death of My Family
Copyright © 2018 Randolph W. Mack. All rights reserved.

All rights reserved. No part of this publication may be reproduced, stored in a retrieval system, or transmitted in any way by any means – electronic, mechanical, photocopy, recording, or otherwise – without the prior permissions of the copyright holder, except by reviewer who may quote brief passages in a review to be printed in magazine newspaper or by radio / TV announcement, as provided by USA copyright law. The author and the publisher will not be held responsible for any errors within the manuscript. All characters appearing in this work are fictitious. Any resemblance to real persons, living or dead, is purely coincidental. Unless otherwise indicated, all scripture quotations are taken from the King James Version of the Bible.

FIRST EDITION
Published in 2019

Author: Randolph W. Mack

Website: www.RWMack.com

ISBN: 978-1-7337299-1-8

Library of Congress Control Number: TXu2-105-136 | July 5, 2018

Category: Biography

Library of Congress Cataloging-in-Publication Data

Editor: Barbara Joe (Amani Publishing LLC)

Proofreader: Kiera J. Northington (itsthewritestuff.com)

Photographer: Eric Bennett

Cover Designer: Barbara Upshaw-Mayers (Aura Graphics and Design)

Publishing Consultant & Formatting: Eli Blyden | EliTheBookGuy.com

Printed & Published in the United States of America

DEDICATION

This book is dedicated to my mother, Mrs. Patricia Green. She was not only the matriarch of our family but also a friend, mentor, spiritual advisor, counselor and an inspiration to others for living.

The love my mom showed her family and friends was only surpassed by the love she had for her Lord and Savior, Jesus Christ. Regardless of the trials she encountered, her faith in God was unwavering; she never questioned Him or complained. She was a pillar of strength whose love for God transcended, simply believing in Him, she knew Him!

I dedicate this book to you to finish what you never got the chance to start. I hope what I'm doing will be acceptable to show how beautiful you were. If I'm able to meet the standard you set as far as your faith in God that all things are possible through Christ, then I know this book will serve as a beacon of light for families to stay closer.

I miss you and love you eternally. The love you showed me, as a parent, is what I try to show my children. God knows I wish they could have met you and been graced with your beauty, strength, calm spirit, and assuring embrace.

You were always my silver lining behind the dark clouds. Thank you for the beautiful experiences and the infinite wisdom you gave me. You were truly virtuous and blessed.

– Love, your son

Table of Contents

DEDICATION iii
INTRODUCTION 1
The Provider 3
She Was Determined.. 9
Her Faith in God 15
The Unifier.. 21
She Tested Positive 27
'Til Death Did They Part 33
When Death Came for Sam 43
Living With HIV: Life After Sam.................................. 49
The Death of The Matriarch 57
The Death of My Family 65
My Brother and Sisters Today 71
Other Families Have Problems Too! 75
In Conclusion.. 81
ACKNOWLEDGMENTS 87

The Death of A Matriarch

The Death Of A Matriarch
The Death Of My Family

Randolph W. Mack

The Death of A Matriarch

INTRODUCTION

This book is an account of my mother's life and the impact it had on our family as the matriarch. It's a story of a woman who endured many hardships and how she emerged on the other side of them through her faith in God.

This book details how determination and persistence led my mom to be able to accomplish all of her goals, as well as how she was a leader to her friends and a light that could illuminate the darkest nights for her family.

This book will also look at my mother's marriage and describe how she took the bitter with the sweet, the ups with the downs, the wrongs with the rights, and even death that comes with life.

Beyond anything, this book will show that regardless of what my mom encountered, her faith in the Lord and her Savior, Jesus Christ, never wavered and nothing could exalt itself beyond the Almighty God to her. You will be able to see how close my family was with my mom and how it has devastated our unity since she left us.

In conclusion, this book will, hopefully, serve as a guide to bring families closer together. Being civil, compassionate, and part of a democracy all comes first from being part of a family, which was essential to my mom.

CHAPTER 1

The Provider

───◆───

As far back as I can remember, I can recall my mother being a provider. This included my childhood and living in the projects. Back then, in the early 70s, a lot of families struggled to eat a basic meal. Although we lived in the projects, we ate like we lived in a penthouse. This stands out because I can remember a lot of my friends having fried baloney sandwiches, mayonnaise sandwiches, and sugar sandwiches. While, at least six days a week, my mother cooked on the stove. There were no microwaves, at least none that I can remember, when I was growing up. A lot of my friends knew we always had food and would often try to get me to sneak them a plate, or ask my mother if they could eat with us.

All of our family and her friends called her Pat; I just called her Mom. She had beautiful coffee-colored skin, stood about five-five, and weighed around 140 pounds. She loved wearing her natural hair in a pretty short style. She always flashed a gorgeous smile with sparkling white teeth, but the most noticeable feature about my mom was her piercing brown eyes. Seemingly, they could see right through me, especially when I was lying.

My mom was married to Lewis, my youngest sister Shelia's father. My oldest sister's name is Tarya; she was raised by our grandmother. My brother's name is Reginald, but we call him Man. Regina is my other sister; she's one year older than me. We all had nice clothes and shoes. Reginald and I got haircuts regularly at the local barbershop to keep us looking fresh. Shelia and Regina kept their hair done in fresh perms.

Although Christmas is supposed to be a fun time for kids, most of the kids in the projects didn't have much to celebrate. Somehow, my mom made a way for all of us to have the things we wanted and even things we didn't ask for that she knew we would love having.

Birthdays were the same way. We all had celebrations on our birthdays. We got a cake, ice cream, and presents. On Easter, we got new outfits for church along with short sets for after church. Halloween was a fun time; we were allowed to transform ourselves into whomever or whatever we wanted with a new costume.

In essence, we had everything we wanted and needed. As I look back on it, the most important thing we had was discipline. At times, it seemed like she was mean; but now I understand that if there had not been structure, we probably would not have the balance to lead our own children. My mom was able to balance discipline and not cross the line of what is considered to be abuse. A lot of my friends were abused by today's standards, which I feel caused some of them to make choices that led to dead-end roads. Some of those roads led to death at early ages, some to drugs and alcohol, and some to doing things that got them put in prison.

While allowing us to be kids and have friends, my mom knew who we played with and either approved of it or made it understood we couldn't play with certain kids. She never believed kids were bad; but she believed if they didn't have an involved parent at home, the children could get in trouble or even be troubled themselves. Not only did I have a healthy fear of getting in trouble, so did my friends when it came to my mom and being in her presence. When my buddies came to my house, they knew they had to be on their best behavior.

My mom was also known to be a comforter to me as well as my brother and sisters, friends and their mothers, who sometimes would be going through problems with their husbands. She could turn the most hostile situation into an opportunity for unity and forgiveness.

All the things my mom provided at home also gave us the stability to do well in school. When I was growing up, how we dressed could get us picked on to the point of feeling tormented. But at the beginning of every school year, we all had new outfits and shoes. Knowing we had new clothes and shoes inspired us to want to go to school.

I know kids nowadays go to school dressed in designer clothes and shoes, but I'm talking about in the 70s when there were no Jordan's, Tru Religion and Polo. It was only Converse All-Stars and K-Mart tennis shoes. This was a time when hand-me-downs were looked at as being like new clothes by some of the kids I grew up with.

Another thing my mom provided for us was an example of respect for her own parents; we affectionately called them Mother and Papa. I never heard my mother disrespect her mother or father. She truly loved them, and they truly loved her. This display served as a standard for us to follow as we grew and brought our children around her. When her grandkids were in her presence, we could tell it was the same admiration we had for our grandparents.

All in all, what she provided was a sense of family.

The Death of A Matriarch

CHAPTER 2

She Was Determined

My mother was always determined to do better than she had already done, not only for us but for herself. My earliest memory of my mom having a job was as a janitor for GTE. Before then, she was a homemaker. Basically, her job was cooking for us, getting us to school, and providing for us while maintaining a functional marriage with Lewis.

At some point, my mom wanted to get a job. I can remember her walking downtown to clean after hours in the offices of GTE. While Lewis worked in the daytime, my mom worked at night. Lewis walked her to work. Being that it was only a few blocks away, sometimes I walked with them. By the time she got off, it would be so late that I would be asleep. But Lewis would be there at her job to walk her back home.

During these walks to and from the job, my mom always talked about wanting to learn how to do the jobs the people in the offices she was cleaning were doing. She always said she could do what they were doing, and she was determined to learn how. At the time, they were called switchboard operators.

Every night she went to work, she asked the women operators questions about how to work the machines and what all the different equipment was called and what purpose it served. As time went on, her determination and confidence grew to the point that when a job opening became available, she filled out an application for the position of a *switchboard operator*. She was given an interview; it involved one's knowledge of the machines and how they functioned. By this time, she not only knew all the functions of the machines, she knew what every part did, and its function collectively and separately. So she was hired to be a switchboard operator. I could tell, even at the young age of twelve or thirteen, she loved working and took pride in her job.

By getting this job, it made her stand out even more among the mothers in the projects, mostly because few of the mothers worked. The majority either had husbands, who were longshoremen like Lewis, or they were receiving government assistance or both. Either way, few of the mothers worked outside of the home.

With her determination to get a job came her determination to move out of the projects. This was a determination that exceeded her desire to work. Not only did she want to move, but she also wanted to become a homeowner. I'm not sure what set my mom on this course; but it was as if she was undergoing a complete transformation to become who, in her mind, she had the potential to become.

I think it all starts with our parents being our first teachers to mold and shape our character. I also believe that despite this, once people reach a certain age, they choose to do right or wrong. My mom, had a virtuous mother and a hard-working father, which helped her keep her values and drive to succeed in check and balanced.

I don't think what she set out to accomplish was a chance occurrence. I truly believe it was a sound choice.

I've heard the saying, "There's no such thing as good luck; but when preparation meets opportunity, dreams can become a reality." My mom prepared herself by getting a job and filing for grants available to first-time homeowners who were single parents. She also saved her money to have what would be the closing costs. So when the opportunity presented itself, she was able to get her a home in the suburbs.

One day, I can remember getting out of school, coming home, and seeing no furniture in our place. I called it our place because it wasn't an apartment, it wasn't a house—so all I could think to call it was a place. I asked my mom, "What happened to everything?"

She replied, "We are moving."

I didn't get a chance to tell my friends bye. To me, it was a big deal because I grew up with them and had known them my whole life. At this point, I was about thirteen years.

My grandfather was there to take us to our new home. Once there, I was surprised, to say the least. My brother and I had our own room, and Gina and Shelia had their own room. We had carpet, the living room was huge, and plenty of room in the dining room. There was a laundry room outside, a carport, and a nice-sized front and back yard. We lived in the middle of the block. Most of our neighbors were African American families, who had found their way from the projects to an apartment or government subsidized housing, one way or another. It was a beautiful neighborhood with plenty of kids our age. People had cars, and there were two convenience stores within walking distance. The school we attended was also within walking distance.

Because it was so nice out there, the transition was smooth. Soon, I had more friends than I'd ever had, and one of them I grew up with in the projects lived only two blocks away.

My mom made a lot of changes in her personal life, as well as our lives. Shortly before we moved, she revealed to me that Lewis was not my biological father. He adopted me and married her shortly after I was born. I was later introduced to Willie, my biological father. However, I still looked at and loved Lewis as my father; I accepted Willie as my dad.

Lewis used to drink a lot. I guess my mom felt his priorities were not in perspective with hers, so not only did we leave the projects, we left Lewis as well.

When we first moved to our home, it was just me, my brother, my two sisters, and our mom. Then it seemed as if Sam came from out of nowhere. Within a short time, he and my mom were married, and he moved in with us. We didn't accept Sam as our father but as our mom's husband. We got along with him. He was nice to our mom and treated her like a lady; he never abused her physically or verbally, and she loved him. So, this is the course we were on as a family. It turned out to be quite a journey; a journey that would involve love, life, and death.

The Death of A Matriarch

CHAPTER 3

Her Faith in God

Growing up, every Sunday was for church. We grew up going to a Baptist church, where my grandparents were members for over twenty-five years. The church happened to be in the projects we lived in. My brother, sisters, and I went "Class A" every Sunday. I would have on a suit with matching tie and shoes, a fresh haircut, and my favorite part was that I was always given money, either change or a dollar bill, to put in the collection tray they passed around. This became my foundation for religion. I believe it was also my mother's beginning.

My grandmother had an unwavering faith in God. My grandfather was likewise. Every Sunday after church, we rode with my grandparents to Kentucky Fried Chicken, got the meal combo bucket of chicken, and went to their home to eat. Then my grandfather, my brother, and I watched wrestling. This was our routine until we moved.

We moved over twenty-five miles from where we'd grown up and where we went to church and even further from our grandparents. So we no longer attended church with them. However, we did continue to go to their house on some weekends and holidays. This is the point I remember my mother's faith in God became something she openly professed and made it a point to institute it into our daily lives. I believe it was always in her and because we were not attending church, we, as a family, became the church. My mother made sure everything involved God and acknowledged him in everything, whether good or bad. Her faith was as if it was an extension of her mother's—unwavering.

Not long after we moved out to our new home, I started getting in trouble. Looking back on it, I realize the more trouble I got in, the more my mom prayed. She believed praying was the answer to all her problems, regardless of how big or small they were.

Every time she prayed about me, I said, "You're putting God on me?"

She would reply, "Son, God is not only on you, but He is in you, too! I'm leaving it in God's hands to deal with you."

It seemed the more she prayed, the worse I got, which caused her to pray more. She even got the ladies she worked with to pray with her for me. They called themselves "prayer warriors." They all worked for GTE; the company she first went to work for as a switchboard operator, which later became Verizon.

They always told me that God loved me. He had something He wanted me to do, and He would not leave me alone until I did it.

I believe I was her "test" as far as her faith went. I watched her evolve into someone who became graceful, had patience, and a firm belief that God's will would be done, regardless of what was happening to make it appear as if it wasn't.

I can remember one day my mother had just prayed about me. I left the house after hearing her preach to me about God's will. I was walking down the street with nowhere to go. All of a sudden, I felt like I was being followed. I looked to my left, and as God is my witness, there was a cloud next to me. Yes, a cloud, just like a thick cloud that's in the sky. I stopped and it stopped. It was right in front of me with what seemed like a thousand twinkling stars in it. I asked, "Why don't you leave me alone and find someone else to do it?"

Do what? I had absolutely no idea. I just remember saying those words. I was terrified and in awe at the same time. I've never forgotten about that. Even though I didn't stop getting in trouble, I feel like that's the point I started to know God was real, and my mom's prayers were being heard. I'm not saying what I experienced was God, but I feel whatever it was, was divine.

As I grew older, I watched my mother's faith mature. As far as she was concerned, everything and all things revolved around God. I noticed she not only prayed with hope but also with confidence. When she prayed about something she truly believed in, it would come out exactly the way she asked for it to happen. This applied to her marriage, children, bills, and anything else.

What came out of this is my unwavering faith in God like my grandmother's, which inspired my mother, and also inspired me. To this day, I grow daily in the Lord and the power of His might. I have four kids now, one daughter and three sons. I pray for them constantly, as my mother prayed for us. I've prayed for some things about them, and I have seen the power and glory of God when my prayers were answered.

I thank God for my mother and her prayers for me; her faith brought me to the knowledge of the truth. While coming to the knowledge of truth, I accepted that all of the saints and prophets endured many hardships. But, they all stood fast to their belief that if God allowed something to befall them, He always provided a way for them to rise above it. With this, I learned to endure my own hardships while believing that God would allow me to be acceptable in His sight and count me as a good soldier of Jesus Christ. 2 Timothy 2:3 instructs us to, "Endure hardship with us like a good soldier of Christ Jesus."

The Death of A Matriarch

CHAPTER 4

The Unifier

My mother was the true matriarch of our family. She single-handedly brought our family together for holidays, birthdays, births, and deaths. Our home in Tampa, Florida, was a neutral gathering spot for all occasions. Regardless of the occasion, my mom made it her business to contact most, if not all of our family. Depending on what it was, she was either a comforter or a coordinator.

Most of our family is concentrated in and around Florida, making it easy to come together. On holidays, we had elaborate cookouts around the pool, including card games for the adults and other games for the children. Most of the time, everyone brought a dish of whatever they felt they specialized in making. My mom and Sam set up tables full of different foods. Sometimes, there would be two or three of the same foods cooked different ways.

Every holiday, even if the out of town family members didn't come, all of us locals would be there. It seemed like everyone showed up, knowing the party would be in full swing at my mom's place.

When it came to birthdays, whether it was one of the kids or an adult, my mom wanted everyone there to sing "Happy Birthday" with a cake and candles—the whole nine yards. We didn't necessarily have to bring presents—that was optional. We were all notified in advance regarding what time the candle lighting would start, and we were expected to be there on time. Even though all we would do was sing "Happy Birthday" and let whoever blow out the candles, it would be disappointing for my mom if someone did not show up without a good reason for not doing so.

This was something she took seriously. To her, it was a special way to let whoever's birthday it was feel that their birthday was truly special and deserved to be acknowledged by everyone in the family, regardless of what the rest of their year was like. She didn't care if we stayed after singing; she just wanted us there when the candles were lit.

She was the same way with births. When someone in the family had a child, my mom was the first one at the hospital and helped the mother out in any way she could.

When the mother was released, she also helped her get settled in at home, and my mom bought things for the baby as well.

After the death of a family member, my mom would take the lead to assist or outright make all the needed arrangements. She took it upon herself to grieve in an introverted way and try to show her strength as the matriarch; the rest of us were able to lean on each other.

She showed this leadership at her mother and father's deaths, as well as when both of Sam's parents passed. She eventually did the same for Sam and had the strength to plan part of her own funeral. She purchased her own burial plot next to Sam's, she told Shelia about her insurance policies, and gave my sister all the documentation to be presented at her death as proof of what was covered and what was to be collected. She even had her will drawn up to disperse all of her assets. I know most responsible adults with property and assets have wills, but it just seemed like my mother didn't do hers as a precaution, but rather as a preparation.

My mom's ability to bring people together extended beyond our family. She was also instrumental in bringing the women she worked with together. They came together when she retired and were the same ladies she worked with for over twenty years. She was one of the founders of what they called the prayer warriors on their job. The term may have been used before they adopted it, but it became a part of their everyday lives.

Whoever was having problems, whether it was personal or professional, the answer for them was always to pray about it. One of their problems became all of their problems. Sometimes it involved children getting in trouble, either in school or at home, and I was one of them. At other times, it involved one of their spouses or even one of the women themselves. Whatever the case, my mom took the lead to resolve it gracefully and never took sides, except for the side of what was right, even if it meant telling her friends they were wrong.

My mom may have helped save some of the women's marriages on more than one occasion. She probably also helped save their children, who may have been messing up in school or with the law or drugs, and even boyfriends or girlfriends.

I can remember my mom always telling her friends, family members, or anyone else, "Don't ask me my opinion if you can't stand the truth. I'm not going to tell you what you want to hear; I'm going to tell you the truth." She said this because people always asked for her advice on how to handle a situation. Knowing people looked to her for this and in this way, never caused her to become arrogant. It made her even more humble. While she knew she had a gift, she also acknowledged that it was a gift from God. Knowing this, she never looked down on anyone or betrayed the trust of anyone who confided in her about serious personal issues.

My mother was a friend to many, a confidante, a counselor, and a minister to others all while being a great mother, grandmother, and a virtuous wife. In all these titles she wore, one of the most important ones was as a unifier.

The Death of A Matriarch

CHAPTER 5

She Tested Positive

Once I found out my mother was positive with the Human Immunodeficiency Virus, or HIV, I was devastated to say the least. Sam, her husband of over twenty years, contracted the virus while cheating on my mother with a young female named Sabrina.

One day, while I was visiting my mother at her home, I decided to ask how she found out she was HIV positive. She told me the details regarding the day she confronted Sam about why he was going to the doctor, because it seemed like every month he needed to have bloodwork done. My mom said, "I got off work and arrived home a little earlier than usual. Sam was in the shower, and I noticed the bag he carried everywhere he went was sitting on the bed. It was the kind of bag some men carried containing a wallet, cologne, cigarettes, keys and small things like that, instead of having loaded pockets. I noticed papers in it, showing Sam had his blood drawn that day. Normally, that would not have been a reason for me to be alarmed. But since it was the third or fourth one I'd seen in the last few months, I naturally became concerned."

I think what caused her to suspect something was wrong, besides the papers and how many times she'd seen them, was the fact Sam never told her he was going to the doctor to have bloodwork done. When one is married, that's not something to keep from a spouse, especially after twenty years of marriage.

"So when Sam got out of the shower, I decided to confront him regarding all the doctor's visits. Before I could ask, Sam noticed his bag had been moved and asked me, "Did you go in my bag? I told him yes, and I want to know why you have been seeing a doctor and having so many blood tests. That's when Sam told me we needed to talk and I screamed at the top of my lungs."

I asked, "What made you do that?"

"My instincts told me what it was."

I questioned further, "How did you know he wasn't going to say something was wrong with only him?"

"The way he looked and the way he said it; I just knew it involved me."

"Did he just come out and say he was HIV positive?" I asked her.

"No, he didn't need to say anything else," my mom replied.

She set an appointment to see her doctor to be tested. The time between her taking the test and waiting for the results was the single most trying time of her life. Eventually, the results came back, confirming her worst fears. Sam had exposed her to HIV.

Here is a woman who didn't smoke, drink, go to bars, or out anywhere for that matter. Her daily life involved going to work and back home. All of a sudden, she's told she has one of the most deadly diseases known to man. It was years before our family knew what was happening with my mom and Sam. But a series of events set things in motion, and it all came out.

First, my mom retired from Verizon after over twenty years of working there. The ladies she worked with had a big retirement party for her. Sheila, Sam, and I attended. Almost all the women who worked in her department, as well as all the other departments, were there.

My mom was popular among her coworkers. She was a confidante to a lot of people there; she gave many spiritual advice and guidance on how to handle situations involving their children or spouses.

After everything unfolded, I found out the real reason she retired was not because she was HIV positive. That was being managed by medications covered by her Blue Cross/Blue Shield, her insurance. Without the medications, she would certainly develop Acquired Immune Deficiency Syndrome, or AIDS, the step past HIV. Without insurance, it could be extremely expensive to get the medications to suppress the virus and prevent it from turning into AIDS. Nor was she sick because other than having the virus, she was healthy. She did not drink or smoke or use drugs, period. So the medications were effective.

The reason she retired was because of Regina, or Gina as we all call her. She followed in my mother's footsteps as far as her job choice. Gina also worked for Verizon. She even worked in the same building with my mother, but on different floors. However, Gina hated my mother and Sam. She accused Sam of trying to molest her at a young age and claimed she told our mother about it, and it went unchecked. She felt my mother chose to believe Sam over her.

Not only that, but she felt our mom chose not to believe her at all. This led Gina to resent our mom more, or at least this was her excuse for it. When it comes to Gina, I cannot understand her, nor do I remember when she started becoming this way. I grew up with her, lived with her, and ate the same food, but I can't seem to remember.

One day, while at work, my mom said she was on the elevator going downstairs on break. The elevator stopped on the floor Gina worked on to pick up some women also going down. When the women stepped in, my mom tuned in to their conversation and overheard one of them say, "It's a shame how she talks about her mom."

My mom didn't have a clue to who they were talking about, until the other one continued, "Right, she said her mom's husband was cheating on her with a girl who recently died of AIDS. He gave her mom the disease, and she's happy because her mother didn't believe her when she told her how he tried to molest her."

My mom nearly fainted upon realizing they were talking about her, and Gina was the girl saying this stuff. At that moment, my mom decided she was going to retire.

What's worse than that is the fact that Christle, the mother of my only daughter, lived next door to the girl Sam was cheating with and exposed him to the virus. Gina knew this, because she and Christle were friends, and Gina frequently visited Christle. Despite hearing rumors that Sabrina, the girl next door had AIDS and seeing Sam over there, Gina never told our mom what was going on. I guess Sam didn't try to hide it; he knew Gina wouldn't say anything to our mom due to the bad feelings she held toward her.

When I first heard this, I remember calling Gina and cussing her out. I called her the worst things I could think of, and I probably thought of some original things to say. To me, the things she said about our mom far exceeded what she accused Sam of attempting to do to her, which was her reason for turning against our mom.

How my mom got past testing positive was beyond my own understanding. Not only did she get past it, but she also held firm to her marriage vows including "for better or worse, sickness and health, 'til death do us part." I believe, with all my heart, the reason she stood by Sam was about more than her marriage vows; it was about her faith in God.

CHAPTER 6

'Til Death Did They Part

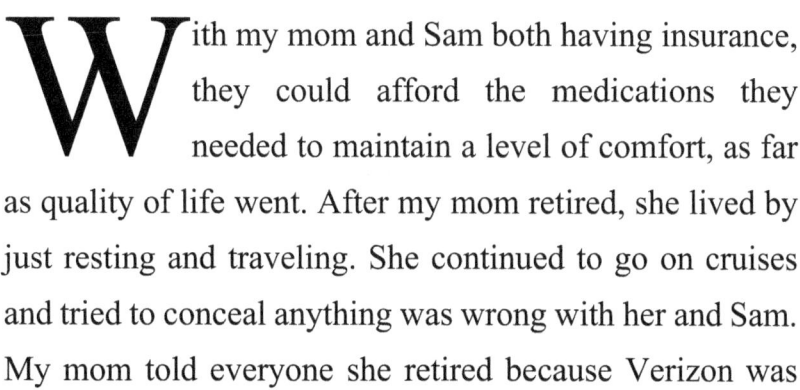

With my mom and Sam both having insurance, they could afford the medications they needed to maintain a level of comfort, as far as quality of life went. After my mom retired, she lived by just resting and traveling. She continued to go on cruises and tried to conceal anything was wrong with her and Sam. My mom told everyone she retired because Verizon was downsizing and offering senior employees the chance to retire with a severance package, so she accepted it.

Soon, it became apparent to us something was wrong when Sam started getting sick and was hospitalized from multiple health complications. At this point, Sam had developed full-blown AIDS.

In his desperate attempt to cure himself, and because of his refusal to accept he was even sick, he stopped taking his medications. Instead, Sam started drinking a "concoction" he was getting from, Dr. Mojo, a man he'd met on the internet. Dr. Mojo told Sam he had a cure for not only HIV, but it was also a remedy for AIDS.

Dr. Mojo convinced Sam this potion had cured dozens of people who had taken it as an alternative to conventional medicines. He convinced him that it was not prescribed as a cure, but rather as a suppressant or stabilizer to prevent HIV from actually becoming AIDS.

In a desperate attempt to get rid of HIV, Sam turned to a desperate measure. There's a saying, "Desperate times call for desperate measures." Sam had accepted this saying to be true.

The reason I said desperate measures is because for this potion to work, it required that Sam stop taking his prescribed medications to be effective. Now Sam said he had read the testimonials of the people claiming to be cured, but it seemed like Sam should have asked to verbally speak to some of these people to verify what he read on the guy's website. All of the stories of people who were cured could have been created by the guy to make his potion seem more credible. It should have been obvious to Sam that if this guy had a cure, it could be verified by people's medical records confirming they were HIV positive, and after being treated with this drink and verifying the virus was eliminated, the entire medical community would have been seeking this man for his natural remedy.

Sam should have also been able to see something was not right when the guy was offering him the drink free of charge. All this guy wanted, in return, was for Sam to endorse his product by saying it cured him without the aid of any other medicine.

With hindsight being 20/20, it's easy to look back and better access the situation. But, that's not something Sam can see looking back because Sam is dead!

When Sam stopped taking his medications to see if the drink would cure him, his HIV status turned into full-blown AIDS. By the time he realized the drink wasn't working and tried to start taking his medicines again, it was too late. He had already started to get sick and had to be hospitalized on several occasions.

My mom told me Sam confronted her about the drink and tried to encourage her to stop taking her medicines with him. She said, "I told him, absolutely, positively—one hundred percent—hell to the no!" My mom repeatedly told Sam not to stop taking his medicines and what Dr. Mojo was saying on his website did not sound realistic. Sam could not be deterred, so he didn't listen to her.

Around this time, the rest of the family started to realize something was wrong with Sam. At first, I thought maybe he had cancer. That thought quickly vanished when I went to visit Sam one day after he had been hospitalized again. This time, I was directed to the floor with all the HIV positive or full-blown AIDS patients. Even then, it did not dawn on me that he was on the AIDS patients' floor.

Looking back on it, I visited Sam three or four times before I accepted he was there because he was infected with HIV or AIDS. What brought me to this reality was the day his doctor came in and informed Sam's nurse about changing his medication for his sexually transmitted disease (STD). I was in total shock because he had been in the hospital almost a month this time. As soon as the doctor left the room, I asked Sam's nurse, "What's really going on with him?"

Before then, it was ask no questions, just be supportive. Now I wanted to know flat out how Sam had gotten an STD while he was in the hospital. When the nurse saw I was ready for the whole truth, she began breaking it all down to me. Sam had full-blown AIDS. He had been HIV positive for several years and had recently developed AIDS as a result of him deciding to stop taking his medications.

As for the STD, when a person gets one, even if it was twenty years ago, it never goes away; it's just dormant after being treated with an antibiotic. But, with a person's immune system being destroyed by the AIDS virus, it all comes back. Every STD Sam had ever been exposed to—even as a teenager—was now back.

I watched this disease literally tear Sam to shreds. It caused him to go totally blind. At times, he was insane. A tube had to be inserted down his throat to assist with breathing. The weight he'd lost was unbelievable, over a hundred pounds.

While all this was going on, thoughts of my mom kept trying to enter my mind; I just refused to entertain them.

One day, I was visiting Sam, and his specialist came to visit him. He introduced himself, and so did I. Dr. Johns stated that Sam was stable and he had been the one treating him and my mother since they both tested positive a few years ago. He shared that if Sam had consulted with him about stopping his prescribed medicines, he would have strongly suggested Sam not do it. Not only because his HIV status could change to AIDS, but the danger would be immediate and irreversible. He was, however, pleased with my mother's viral load currently being undetectable. The viral load is the standard by which the virus is measured. It just means it's at the lowest point of this standard of detection.

After listening to Dr. Johns, I nearly needed him to treat me for what I thought was a heart attack. Somehow, I maintained my composure until he left. Once he did, and I started to breathe again, I looked at Sam only to see he was already looking at me; this was before he went blind and lost his ability to speak. We just stared at each other with tears in our eyes. Out of the silence, I uttered, "I love you."

He responded, "I'm sorry. I love you, too." I just left it at that.

Instantly, my mind turned to who, what, when, where, and how?

When I left the hospital that night, I sat in my truck for what seemed like fifteen or twenty minutes. In reality, it was almost four hours. What was I thinking? I have absolutely no idea. I did know I wanted to confront my mom about what the doctor said about her and Sam.

Eventually, I dialed her number and stated I was getting ready to leave the hospital after visiting Sam. She stated she had gone earlier that morning. I told her I'd met his specialist, and she became silent.

I said, "He's pleased that your medications have been working extremely well for you." She remained silent.

"Mom, I love you and Sam. I will be there for both of you." I detected she was crying, and I was doing the same. Neither of us spoke for what seemed like days. I finally found the strength to say, "Mom, I'm on my way. I will see you when I get there."

"Okay, baby."

When I pulled into her driveway, I saw her sitting at the dining room table, looking out the window like she was waiting for me. I noticed her go toward the door, so I got out of my truck and went toward her. By the time I reached her, we were both crying again. I embraced her to comfort and give her my strength. I held her face in my hands, looked straight into her eyes, and said, "I love you with all my heart, and everything will be fine."

Eventually, we went inside, sat at the table, and I decided I would not ask any questions. I would listen and let her tell me what she wanted me to know. When she was comfortable, she started telling me everything. She began talking about how she first found out after questioning Sam about his going to the doctor so much. She moved on to how she was told by her own doctor about her positive results. Next, she told me about why she retired because of Gina. Then, she confirmed what I already knew, which was she never cheated on Sam. So there was no question the disease came from him. I asked her if there was a possibility it could have happened through tainted blood he received for one reason or another. She said neither one of them had been to a hospital or doctor in years for anything, other than routine check-ups. Using his past check-ups as a measuring stick and timeline, Sam was able to pinpoint when he became exposed.

Sam was employed as a longshoreman and traveled to Texas to train new employees with other guys from Florida. While he was up there, he met Alice, another woman he became involved with. It later came out he was living with her while he was in Texas. His trips there were frequent and lasted for months at a time.

Sam not only infected my mom, but he also infected Alice. Apparently, she knew Sam was married. I'm sure she saw my mom calling daily and probably wrote my mom's phone number down as insurance in case Sam decided to leave her. Anyway, Alice called my mom and told her what had been going on with them. However, when she called my mom, she was not only mad that Sam stopped answering her calls, she had also been sick and went to her doctor only to be told she was HIV positive, too. This set my mom back two steps from the one she had taken forward.

While Sam was in the hospital dying, my mom stuck with her marriage vows, only to hear from another woman that he was not just seeing Sabrina but also this Alice woman in Texas. Instead of going off on the woman and telling her that was what she deserved, my mother, being the saint she was, prayed for her. Alice thought she was going to tell my mom to be careful and reveal how she tested positive for HIV, only to be informed that my mom had also been exposed to the virus by Sam.

My mom tried to tell Sam about her conversation with Alice. By this time, he was only a fragment of himself and death had called him to step forward. It was just a matter of God saying, "That's enough," before he was gone.

I went through a phase of seriously considering killing Sam for what he'd done to my mother. I felt like I was supposed to get revenge for her. But my mom's undying love for Sam, her unwavering faith in God's will, followed by my love for both of them far exceeded any bad thoughts I had and in turn, eliminated any negative feelings I had toward Sam.

Death eventually claimed Sam, and my mom was left to deal with life on her own. My sister and I were there for her, constantly assuring our mom that we loved her and would be there for her.

The Death of A Matriarch

CHAPTER 7

When Death Came for Sam

———◆———

I remember the day Sam passed. I was home and got a call from Sheila. She had become our mother's constant companion and primary caregiver. When I answered the call, I instantly knew something wasn't right. Sheila sounded like she was trying not to cry. Considering the circumstances, even though she had become stronger than most people ever do in their life at such a young age, she couldn't help but cry when she told me Sam had just passed. My first question was, "Where is Mom?"

She replied, "Standing right next to me."

"Okay, I will be there in ten minutes," I said, although I lived twenty minutes away.

My mom had just returned from attending my niece Dashia's graduation in Atlanta, Georgia. She wanted to attend the graduation to try to have a sense of normalcy, despite everything that was going on. At this time, most of us knew what her and Sam's condition really was. She didn't want the ones who didn't know what was going on to figure it out from her giving any reason not to attend the ceremony, because one of my mom's mottos was, "Education is essential."

She decided to go after Sheila and I encouraged her to by saying Sam would be okay until she returned. Also, Angie, Sam's daughter, and I promised we would be there for him until she returned.

The day my mom left, she called to say that she and Sheila had made it safely to Atlanta. Later that night, I told her to relax and enjoy herself; everything would be fine.

About two hours later, I received a call from Angie at the hospital visiting with Sam. She screamed, "They just called a *code blue* on Sam!" A code blue is a term used by hospitals to alert hospital staff that someone is dying. A group called a code team is supposed to respond to the patient's room number that was called.

I remember dropping to my knees and praying out to God. As long as I can remember, I've heard it said, "He would not put more on us than we could handle."

I told God that my mom had put a lot into going to the graduation and did not want to leave Sam's side; she wanted to be there with him in his last moments. She knew

Sam could be leaving any day at any time because his health had gotten critical. I said, "Your Word has sustained my mom her whole life. It would be too much on her if Sam died now while she's away, especially on the same day she left."

While I was praying, Angie was still on the phone. I didn't even realize it until I opened my eyes and noticed I still had the phone in my hands. I put the phone to my ear and heard Angie say, "He's stabilized again."

All I could say was, "Thank You, God."

I told Angie, "Sam will be fine until my mom makes it back home in a couple of days."

To this day, I feel that was the turning point in my life when I went from believing to knowing—knowing God was a living being, who could hear our prayers, show mercy, and tell death to stand down. I also knew His words were true that He wouldn't put more on us than we could handle. Even while I acknowledged how powerful God could be, I didn't fully grasp the scope of what happened until much later in my life. It was too enormous for me to wrap my mind around when it first happened.

Sam remained stable, but still critical, for the next few days. My mom returned that Monday morning. She and Shelia went to the hospital later that day to be with Sam, and that's the day he went code blue again. This time, he didn't make it. So God allowed my mom to be with Sam the way she wanted to be in his last moments. As soon as he passed, I got the call from Shelia, and I was there in what seemed like ten minutes.

As if it were yesterday, I can recall reaching the floor Sam was on and turning the corner to see my mom and Sheila standing outside his room. The look on my mother's face will forever be etched in my mind. It was the saddest look I have ever seen on a human being in my life. It broke my heart. At that moment, I embraced her and tried to comfort her the best I could. I looked at Shelia, and she looked distressed as well. After holding my mom and assuring her that God would be with her to strengthen her, I turned to Sheila and said, "You've got to be strong for Mom."

Eventually, I walked into the room and saw Sam lying on the bed, dead. It seemed surreal to see him like that. He looked like he was only taking a nap. His eyes were partially opened. I just stood there staring at him as if I expected him to inhale or exhale. Instantly, I realized I was in the presence of death.

By this time, Angie had arrived. I stepped out of the room to greet and console her. Sam and Angie were close;

she was his baby girl. So, she took it hard when he passed. I asked her, "Do you want to go in the room?"

She said, "Yes."

As soon as we entered the room, Angie looked up, saw Sam, and dropped like a sack of rocks. I had to catch her to stop her from hitting the ground. She'd passed out. When she regained consciousness, she was hysterical. I felt helpless trying to comfort three women at the same time.

In time, we pulled ourselves together and found solace in each other. We all left the hospital and headed to my mother's home, where the rest of the family came as they got the news about Sam.

The Death of A Matriarch

CHAPTER 8

Living With HIV: Life After Sam

My mom was faced with the responsibility of making all the arrangements for Sam's funeral. She decided it was time to reveal to the rest of the family what really claimed Sam's life, while at the same time revealing her own condition.

I think a lot of my relatives had formed some opinion about what they thought was wrong with my mom and Sam. Although my mom never said what the problem was, she also never said what it wasn't, which left room for speculation. Besides that, Sam had been in and out of the hospital on a few occasions because of different complications, and in looking back on it now, when we see someone admitted into a hospital, we can be sure something is wrong. The way hospitals operate nowadays, if you're not seriously ill or hurt, you're treated as an outpatient.

My mom was admitted to the hospital once. She was eating chicken and accidentally swallowed a small piece of a bone, and it scratched the lining of her throat. She nearly bled to death. The amount of blood she received through transfusions was equal to all the blood in her body. As the blood was put in her, it ran back out, all from the scratched throat. She was in intensive care for over a month on a respirator.

We were told on several occasions, by her team of doctors, she was not going to make it. But, as if touched by the hands of God, the scratch healed and the transfusion finally worked. Even though that was the only time my mom was hospitalized for anything relating to HIV, it almost took her life. So this is why I said I feel some of my relatives suspected something was seriously wrong. It's unusual to see two married people, who had never been sick in over twenty years, both become deathly ill at the same time without an explanation.

As my mother and Sheila made contact with Sam's relatives, coworkers, friends, and members on our side of the family, the news of his death was shocking and unexpected by most of them. Most of the family was easy to contact and assured my mother they would be there for the funeral.

The one person my mom was not able to contact was her brother, Warren. Warren had just left Florida after visiting my mother and Sam in the hospital two weeks before Sam passed. He wanted to come down to visit them before he went on an extended vacation. My mom and Sheila tried nonstop for days to reach Warren. But every time they called, his phone went straight to voicemail. With Sam's funeral fast approaching, my mother's attempts to reach Warren became more urgent. We did not have another number to try to reach him nor did we have a number to his girlfriend or anyone else living in the area, which was in some part of Alabama in the backwoods section.

On the day of Sam's funeral, we still had not made contact with Warren. This caused my mom a lot of stress, because Warren was her only sibling and both of their parents were deceased. The rest of the family was present at the funeral. It was a sad occasion for all of us, especially my mom. All of Sam's friends and coworkers were there, as well our respective families. Everyone tried to console my mom; it was obvious she was far beyond words mending her.

We got through the funeral and Sam was laid to rest. He was buried in the same cemetery as my maternal grandparents. So, while she was dealing with burying Sam, she was reminded of her parents buried just a stone's throw away from his grave. Not only that, the empty plot next to Sam was the place my mom purchased for herself to be buried when she passed away. We were sitting and standing on it while Sam's funeral was taking place. She even commented that she would be right there soon, pointing at the spot as we were leaving.

The first thing my mom wanted to do when we all got back to her home was to try to contact Warren again. She was still unable to make contact for the next several days.

Finally, she called Warren's phone, and someone answered. She asked if Warren was available and explained how she had been desperately trying to reach him. My mom was told that Warren had been in the hospital the whole time she had been trying to call, and his phone was with his property at the hospital. She found out Warren was admitted for food poisoning, but while he was there, he contracted a staph infection. It's something people usually catch while in the hospital. The staph infection Warren had was incurable and proved to be deadly; it claimed his life two days after my mom made contact with his wife.

This was devastating to my mother because she had not even begun to deal with her husband's death only to be told her only brother was now dead two weeks later. We made plans to attend Warren's funeral just three weeks after Sam's. During this time, I saw my mom age what seemed like a hundred years in less than a month. She cried; she was sad and heartbroken. At the same time, her faith in God was still unwavering. She may have bent a little, but she never broke. She may have leaned to the left a little, but she always leaned back to the right. Shelia, my mom, and I caught a plane to Alabama for the funeral. Even I was worn out from dealing with the losses, while having the thoughts of my mother being next on my mind. The funeral was a repeat of Sam's. My mom was crushed. I prayed to God to have mercy on her because it seemed she couldn't take anymore. It seemed like my mom had gotten to the point where she would have welcomed death. She just wanted to stop hurting. It was just one thing after another, and it seemed like it kept getting worse.

I got to the point where I stopped telling her it would be okay; I started telling her that I loved her and Shelia and I would be there for her no matter what.

After Warren's funeral, we flew back to Tampa. At this time, Shelia was living with our mom although she had her own home. My mom would also stay at Shelia's for extended periods, as well as stay with me to give Shelia a break.

Shelia and I tried to comfort our mom as much as possible while she sorted out things in her own way and in her own time. Being the strong woman she was, along with her faith in God that He would not put more on her than she could bear, she eventually started to regain her composure and told me God's grace was sufficient and enough to sustain her. She stayed on top of taking her medications, and her viral load remained undetectable. Her appetite was like a lion; she loved to eat and was a true connoisseur of good food. Shelia and I made sure she had everything she wanted for breakfast, lunch and dinner, including all kinds of snacks. Not only was this good to her, but it was also good for her as well. It was important for her to eat and keep her immune system as strong as possible. So when our mom did come to my home, I cooked all her favorite dishes or got something from her favorite restaurants.

This became routine for my mom. She was being taken care of by us; well, primarily Shelia. Going to her doctor for check-ups, relaxing, eating the best food, and watching *The Golden Girls* television show. There wasn't much she wanted to do if it involved being outside the house. In spite of all the people she supported through their trials, there were none to be found when it came down to who was supportive of her. Except, my beautiful sister, Shelia, and me. All in all, the women she worked with for over twenty years and had established friendships deep enough to call themselves prayer warriors—only a few stayed in touch with her, and some I knew she was really close to didn't support her at all.

Regardless of who stood by my mother, her only concern was to one day be in the presence of God, whom she loved with all her heart.

My brother, Sam's two daughters, Nikki and Angie, whom my mother raised; my two other sisters, Tarya and Gina, along with Tarya's daughter, also named Nikki, whom my mother raised from the day she was born (and everyone thought was our sister because she had been with us her whole life), none of them gave my mom support. If they did, it was when they felt like it, which was far and few times in between. Still, between the two of us, Shelia and I made up for all of them, and for what they didn't have time for.

My mom didn't let it bother her about who did or didn't stand by her. She had been through so much behind the deaths of Sam and Warren, and her own condition until nothing could move her to the left or right.

The Death of A Matriarch

CHAPTER 9

The Death of The Matriarch

When my mother died, it was sudden and unexpected. She actually died on the cruise ship *Imagination*, which is part of Carnival Cruise Lines. My mom and Sheila went on many cruises. I don't think there is an island they have not visited. For twenty years, this was a passion for her. My mom and Sheila had to reschedule the trip several times, because my mom was not feeling well when the time would come for them to leave. So, she really wanted to make it this time.

I dropped her and Sheila off so they could depart. Everything went smoothly as far as getting there on time and to the right place for their ship. We said goodbye, and we would see each other in a few days.

I went home and got into my normal routine. Everything was fine, until I received a phone call later on that night from Sheila. When I first looked at the caller ID on my phone and saw it was her, it didn't dawn on me that she was calling as if she was local again. But in a split second, it came to me in the form of a question. *How did she get back home?*

So when I answered, my first question was, "How are you calling me from home?"

There was a slight pause, and she said, "I am home."

"Where's Mom?"

Calling me by the nickname my mom gave me because I weighed ten pounds at birth, Sheila said, "Muscle, she's gone."

"Gone where?"

"Muscle, she passed on the ship not long after it left."

I dropped in the spot I was standing. The only thing I could think of was how and from what. And again, where was she? Sheila explained that because she died in international waters, she had to stay on the ship until it went on its course and returned to U.S. territory. At this point, Sheila didn't know what caused her death, because she was doing well as far as her HIV status and on her last check-up, which was less than thirty days before their scheduled trip; her viral load was still undetectable. Being that HIV to AIDS is a progressive disease, I felt it was caused by something other than that. Eventually, it was confirmed that a diabetic reaction caused her death.

The ship was scheduled to return to the United States the following Saturday in Miami, Florida. At that time the funeral home, which was already pre-arranged to handle everything in the event of her death, would pick her up from there and return her to Tampa for burial.

Sheila and I stayed on the phone for a long time. We were saying the same things over and over about how we couldn't believe it. Sometimes during our conversation, I tried to regain my composure so I could be strong for my sister. But, no matter how much I tried or wanted to, she had to lift me.

To me, it was too much to absorb. I couldn't accept that my mom was gone. She was not only my mother; she was also my friend, confidante, spiritual advisor, counselor, and inspiration for my faith in God.

I loved my mother with all my heart. I never disrespected her, ever. By being blessed to have her as my mother, I was able to experience what true, unconditional, unmeasured love is. Not only did I truly love her, but she also loved me as well. So it took me awhile to accept that she was gone. The time extended far beyond our conversation which eventually ended.

Sometimes to this day, almost eighteen years later, I still find myself imagining what it would be like if she was still here, or how she would have handled this or that, and even how different things would be for my kids and me. Either way, one thing is for sure, if she were still here, our family would still be a family, and she would still be the one bringing us all together to remind us of that.

When the cruise ship returned to Miami, the funeral home was there to meet them and claim my mother's body. We had the wake a few days later, before the actual funeral. I can remember it as if it was just yesterday. When I walked into the building she was in, I passed many of her friends and family members. Some appeared to be speaking to me and saying things to get my attention. Some were even trying to approach me, but I couldn't hear them. I avoided them because the only thing on my mind was reaching my mom. When I finally entered the room, I looked straight at her and said, "There you are."

From a distance, I could clearly see her, and I didn't take my eyes off of my mom. I approached her casket, looked down on her, and noticed she had the most peaceful facial expression I had seen on her in years. She looked as if she was younger and stronger than she had been in years. It felt as if the heavens opened for a second, and I heard her say in a strong voice, "I'm okay, baby."

I said, "Thank You, my Lord."

As I stood there transfixed, it was like I was in the spirit. Within what seemed like seconds that transcended time, I saw different events in my life involving my mother and me. Some were of laughter, some of joy, some of when she was going through her struggle with being infected with HIV, while other moments were of her giving me advice and praying for me, but it all led up to the smile I could see emanating from within her.

My mother and I had a special relationship. I knew when I heard her speak to me that love surpasses even death itself.

The funeral was a few days later; it seemed as if everyone in our family found the time to show up. Even the women she worked with and gave her support to when they needed it, showed up. It seems everyone found the time to come shed a tear in her death when none of them had the time to share a smile with her while she was alive.

Her funeral went smooth as planned. From the church, we were led to the cemetery where my grandparents and Sam already were buried. The funeral procession led us right next to Sam's grave.

When my mom took her vows with Sam, she meant it. Her vows had said in sickness and health, for better or worse, and even 'til death parted them. Here we were, about to bury her next to Sam. To me, that was another example of how love surpasses even death itself. As in life, so was she even when faced with death; she loved Sam.

After the funeral, we all gathered at my mother's residence like we had on so many other occasions. I wanted to speak out and say the funeral was over, so they could stop faking like they cared and go home or to hell for all I cared, because of the way they all abandoned her in her time of grief. But, I knew in my heart that would have been the last thing my mom would have wanted me to do. So I held my tongue about that, said goodbye to everyone, and I left.

I guess the reason I was feeling that way was because when I went to the hospital after Sam died and saw the look of pure hurt on my mom's face, it compelled me to want to protect her from anyone or anything that could put her back in that position again. I knew the way everyone turned their backs on her when they found out what was wrong with her and what had taken Sam's life, had deeply hurt my mom. But, as adults, we know when we've done something or someone wrong, so I didn't need to tell them they were wrong for how they treated her. They already knew it.

When my mom died, it seemed my entire family died. I don't think there's been a big gathering since she left. Even with my three sisters and my brother, the only one I'm close to is Shelia. The love our mother had for us transformed itself in us and lives in us through her spirit, even to this day. Yes, I love my brother and other sisters, but Shelia and I are close to each other the way our mom was to us. I don't know of any two other family members who are the same way.

The Death of A Matriarch

CHAPTER 10

The Death of My Family

I can't remember one family get-together since my mother passed where everyone showed up, which mean near and distant relatives.

No occasion has been enough to motivate a reunion, whether it was a birthday, a holiday, a birth, or even a death.

The main reason it has not happened is because there is no longer a leader in the family with the influence to persuade everyone to attend. The closest thing to my mother, as far as influence goes, is Sheila. If she took it upon herself to do it, I believe she could easily become the matriarch.

Sheila has some of the same qualities, attributes, and characteristics our mom had. She's very determined, focused, serious, and persuasive. While at the same time, she's understanding, compassionate, spiritual, and believes in family unity.

However, the differences between the two of them are what make their approach to family contrast. My mother had it in her blood to be this way; Sheila was nurtured by my mother to be like this. My mother did it instinctively; Sheila has to take it upon herself to do it.

There have been times on holidays when she's suggested we get together and "break bread," and the four of us would get together at one of our homes. On these occasions, we would come together, eat, and go our separate ways. It never included our out of town relatives, but there weren't many of them anyway. My mom only had one brother and no sisters, so it was not like there were a lot of aunts and uncles and cousins to begin with. My grandparents didn't have a lot of siblings, either. I don't remember meeting anyone from my maternal grandfather's family. I can only remember meeting one of my maternal grandmother's sisters and a couple of her cousins.

The family we did have was all brought together, first by our grandmother, and then my mom. If something were to happen to someone in our family today, whether good or bad, I'm not sure if anyone would even know how to inform everyone. The reason is that I don't think there's anyone in our family with everyone's contact information to do it. I'm sure this member would know how to reach another one and that one could reach another one and eventually everyone would be contacted. When my mother was alive, it didn't matter if it were a cousin or a child of one of the adults or someone who married into our family, if anything happened to anyone, to her, it was family, and no one was greater than anyone else. Everyone was special simply because they were a part of the family.

At this point, I know of nothing that's happened as far as losing any member of our family. I hope that if anything does happen, whether good or bad, that somehow we, as a family, will come back together. Hopefully, we can turn back to what has sustained us through life's ups and downs, as well as the ins and outs through prayer and unity. Growing up, I always heard people say, "A family that prays together, stays together." While this will not prevent a family from experiencing trials, it will provide a support system that will strengthen a family regardless of who's lost or whatever is gained.

In experiencing the way our family was, compared to how it is now, I can only ask a question. Did my mom have that much influence to bring our family together single-handedly? Or was she only able to do it because she was the only one in the family who took it upon herself to initiate unity, and everyone went along with it to be nice rather than just saying no to getting together on holidays and other occasions? I guess we can only say no for so long when someone keeps trying to invite us to something that involves our own family. Sooner or later, they will see we don't want to be involved. My mom would not just call and request our presence; she was relentless as if it was one of her reasons for living. With all the energy and effort she put into our family being close, it seemed it would have been enough to keep our family together for generations. While at the same time, it seems someone should have taken on the role of being the matriarch or patriarch of the family. It's hard to imagine that a family that's always had a leader could so easily fall apart.

Maybe this book will inspire Sheila to accept her calling and bring our family back to the point it was. She's the only one with the "juice" to make it happen. Since my mother passed, there's been multiple children born into our family. I have added three sons since my mom passed. Sheila has had a son and my niece, Nikki, has had another son. I'm sure there have been many others who will never even know each other if the adults don't take it upon ourselves to unite them.

Besides loving the atmosphere of being with our direct family members, it was always something I looked forward to when I was with my male cousins and could see the resemblance between us in the way we looked, dressed, talked, and walked. Even though we were from different cities and states, we were built alike and had some of the same good and bad habits. Bottom line, we were all blood in and blood out—family.

No one seemed to get more out of the reunions than my mom. I can remember how I could be talking to my male cousins, when we would maybe be out front at one or the other's car drinking, talking, or whatever, and I would notice my mom moving from one part of the house to another. Our eyes would lock on each other; I could see she was on cloud nine from seeing everyone laughing, smiling, and having a good time. I would wink my eye at her; she would wink back with a smile from ear to ear.

Her favorite part of the get-togethers was when it was time to gather around the table and with everyone holding hands, say our thanks to God for the food as well as the family. Once the feast started, she would not stop moving until everyone was so full from eating that we couldn't move. She always made sure there was enough of everything, and everyone had enough.

When it was time for everyone to go home, my mom would always send them on their way with a reminder of when the next event or holiday would be. My mom expressed how she not only wanted them there, but expected them to be there.

I truly miss my mom, as well as the unity she inspired in our family.

CHAPTER 11

My Brother and Sisters Today

All of my mother's children are still alive, and all of us are over fifty. Tarya, is the oldest; then my brother we call Man; then there's Gina; then the baby, Shelia, and myself. I would say we talk to each other on occasions that sometimes bring us together at one or the other's house. This only happens two or three times a year at the most.

Shelia and I, on the other hand, stay in constant contact. It's as if Shelia has filled the void my mother left in regards to me having someone I could talk to about any and everything from females to finances. Regardless of what it was, she always displayed the virtue and balance between right and wrong in the same meticulous way my mom did when someone asked her for advice.

If the drive my mom had for unity in our family could be seen after she passed within anyone in our family, Shelia and I would be the symbols of that success.

Today, Tarya or T. as we call her is 58 and doing good. She has her own place and most of the time she's working two or three jobs at the same time. I would describe her as a survivor. Although she has made some bad choices in life, she found a way to turn it all around and come out on top. T. is all about treating you the way you act. Meaning if you show her you care she will show you even more of the same, but if you let her see you don't care about her she will let it be clear that she's not going to go out of her way to change your mind and she will just shut down on you. But all and all she is a good person and all about family and being close.

Reginald, or Man as we call him is 55 and a retired Air Force Veteran that served over 20 years of active duty. After retiring he still works for the Air Force in a civilian capacity. My brother is a standup, no nonsense kind of person. He lives on the east coast of Florida and besides his job, he owns a Day Care Center. He's married and owns a beautiful home. Even when we were young boys it seems like my brother was a grown man. His character was that of being mature beyond his age. He was very smart in school and never got into trouble as a youth.

Growing up I think me and my brother loved each other and to this day I feel we still do and we respect each other as Men. We talk when we talk and when we do it's with laughter and love. I think he is an all-around good dude and I love having him as my big brother, my only brother.

Regina or Gina as we call her is 54. Gina retired from Verizon and now owns a clothing store She's also married and owns her home. Me and Gina are cool and we also talk when we talk. She is driven and dances to her own beat. Gina can be nice as an angel, or as mean as a hornet if you get on her wrong side. She is the best cook in the family. We all know how to cook and each one of us has a dish we specialize in but hands down she's the queen of the kitchen.

As far as what went on with her and our mom. When I first heard it, I hated her and cussed her out in several languages. But as time has a way of doing what it does, I decided that that's between her, our mom and All Knowing, All Seeing, and Almighty God!

Shelia is the baby of us all. When I say baby, she is a old baby LOL. She's 51. Shelia is married and owns a beautiful home not far from my home. She owns 3 rooming houses, at least 2 Day Care Centers and a couple of rental properties. She is the heir to being the Matriarch of our family. Shelia is the most loyal person I know in this world. If she's on your side there is nothing she would not do for you. The love and support she gave our mom came naturally to her. Not only to my mom, but me as well and beyond that my kids just as much.

I swear, I never saw her flinch when it came to taking care of our mother. I think Shelia would be more motivated to be the Matriarch of our family if everyone showed some interest in first being a family. But with the way things are today with social media, people would rather "like a post" than say hello. Or text instead of dialing your number

Shelia has the same demeanor as we all do, which is "I care if you do". That is a description of my siblings and where they are at in life today. Could we all be closer? Yes. And God willing we will get there.

CHAPTER 12

Other Families Have Problems Too!

This generation of families is different from how families were when I was growing up. The most obvious difference is the age of the parents, grandparents, and great-grandparents. When I was coming up, all the grandparents were elderly; they had been together for what seemed like forever. They had wisdom, leadership abilities, were respected by their children, and were involved in their grandchildren's lives.

Now they are mothers at fifteen. By thirty, they are grandmothers and by forty-five, they are great-grandmothers. The problem with this is a lot of women and men are not becoming truly mature until they reach their forties and fifties. Some people, in this new approach, believe fifty is the new forty. Forty is the new thirty, and thirty is the new twenty. I guess that makes twenty like ten? I don't know how it got like this. The older people are acting young while the younger generation is acting older.

When I was growing up, I remember my family, as well as most everyone I grew up with, went to church every Sunday with our grandparents. Our grandparents were involved in our lives, in general, including school, holidays, and birthdays. My grandfather did things with my brother and me. That was the basis of turning boys into men. He taught us how to paint, cut grass, drive, and how to use different tools. Just the way he carried himself was an example to me, as it was to my siblings. My grandmother was a strong, virtuous woman. She carried herself with a display of grace and elegance, whether she was home or at church. Despite my grandfather being a dominant force in our family, it was clear my grandmother was the matriarch.

As children, we followed my mother's examples of how she had reverence for her parents and showed the same affection to them as my mother did. For Shelia and I, it even invoked a level of respect for our own mother that, to this day, has transcended even in her death.

True love is infinite and surpasses depths, heights, darkness, light, death, and life itself. I know this because the love I had for my mother when she was alive is physically the same measure of love I have for her now spiritually. It's the same for Shelia, who frequently visits our mother's gravesite. She also commemorates our mom's birthdate every year, as well as Mother's Day and the anniversary of her death in our local newspaper.

I think the biggest way Shelia shows the love she has for our mother is the way she truly loves everyone in our family. She also has a level of compassion and forgiveness that comes from her "still spirit" and faith in God. This is why I said in the earlier chapter that Shelia is the link and, if placed in the right position, she could bring our family back to the place and point it was at when our mother was alive. Her experience from our grandmother, mother, and seeing how they functioned in our family in combination with her own experience in being a leader and a lady, she has the most potential to become the next matriarch in our family.

With a lot of this generation's families, there was never a real example of leadership. A lot of the children are more friends with their parents rather than having a parent/child relationship. There are some thirty-year-old mothers with fifteen-year-old daughters whom one would see and think they were sisters. It may be the clothes or the way the mother presents herself that makes her indistinguishable from her daughter. There are even some thirty-year-old daughters with forty-five-year-old mothers, and we can't tell which one is the parent.

The grandmothers today go clubbing like they are still twenty. Some go out with their children. Believe it or not, there are even some grandparents going out with their grandchildren. The girls, in a lot of these families, see not only their mothers going out with different men, some are out with younger men. They also see their grandmothers doing it. So it's not hard to figure out why the cycle is not broken.

The grandmothers today are not into keeping their grandchildren. Some won't because they want to go out on the weekends just as much as their daughters. Some don't keep their grandchildren because they have some man they don't want to be inconvenienced by having children on the weekend. They may consider it as their off days from work, or the man wants the grandmother's undivided attention on the weekends.

Some grandparents consider their grandchildren to be bad and feel like having them over may cause their things to get broken, or things will have to be rearranged.

Some grandparents don't like being involved with their grandchildren because they feel like it will cost them money one way or another. I know times are harder than usual, but I don't feel they are any harder than they were thirty or forty years ago. Back then, grandparents always gave grandchildren a few dollars for having good school report cards. They made sure the kids had Easter baskets, even if they made them at home. They would start getting Christmas gifts as early as October, to make sure something would be under the Christmas tree.

Even in the summer, the grandparents would get short sets for the kids for family picnics. They would not only help with their grandkids; they would help their own children if they needed it. The grandfathers were the backbone of these families; they stood silently beside or behind their wives and let them call the shots while they enforced them.

Nowadays, the grandparents will barely help their grandkids with a backpack for school. The parents could be struggling with a light bill, water bill, car payment, or rent, and they are out of luck if they need help from their parents, even if they have grandchildren.

This is not to say all grandparents are this way today. It is the way the majority of families are, though. There is no unity. There is no more everyone coming together if someone in the family needs something where the entire family would chip in to meet what the need was, even if someone had the misfortune of going to jail, everyone would come together.

The biggest change that's had the biggest impact on the state of families today is the lack of a spiritual leader. A lot of young parents don't go to church; a lot of these young parents are grandparents and don't insist on their grandchildren attending church every Sunday with them if they do go.

The first step to restoring the unity families once had is to put God first again. When this is done, everything else will fall in place. Just like the saying we've all heard, "A family that prays together, stays together".

In Conclusion

For my family, as well as other families, to be restored to their former glory, someone will have to step up and assume the leadership role, regardless if it's a male or a female. Whoever it is will have to be someone respected by the entire family; someone who has consistently displayed the ability to solve problems in a calm and temperate manner. Also, someone who has a spiritual base is needed. It will take a person who has respect in their own house, meaning with their husband/wife and kids if they have any.

More than likely, it will take a female in the family to be the example and matriarch. Not one who listens to more rap music than the children in the family; not someone who will borrow one of their grandchildren's CDs of a rapper who is both of their favorites, or someone who doesn't wake up until church is over on Sunday mornings because she's been out partying all night. The family cannot be led by a grandmother who dresses like she's a teenager, especially if she dates a teenager or one who smokes or drinks with the grandkids or her kids.

The reason I feel it will be a female is because a lot of men are just not into their own grandchildren the way they used to be. This applies to African Americans, in particular, but certainly is not limited to them. A lot of middle-aged men are more into video games than their children. A lot of men are not involved with their children at all because they hate the mothers, or they have let child support cause them not to want to be involved. Because they hate paying child support, they feel like their children are more of a liability than an asset, and the males today are just downright immature, and can't lead themselves past the zippers on their own pants. There are males today not truly becoming men until they are pushing fifty, and some never fully grow up. The reason I made the statement about African Americans is because so many of us are incarcerated in America. That's not to say it's because of this that they are excluded from being a part of their family. I do, however, believe that leaders lead by example. This is impossible to do if one is incarcerated because one is then forced to follow rather than lead.

Some women are faced with the responsibility of playing the roles of mother and father because of the father's incarceration or simple lack of involvement. While some females are immature and don't have their priorities in perspective to being a role model for their children, they still seem to settle down quicker than most men. Some grow up being responsible as do some men. It's just more often that it's the women bringing and keeping their families together.

What's going to have to happen to make families the way they once were is someone is going to have to care! Someone is going to have to make a difference. If it doesn't matter to anyone whether they are a close family, then more than likely, no one will take it upon themselves to put forth the effort to unify the family. If the children of the family grow up not seeing unity among the adults, they will not inherit the belief that family unity is vital.

To some families, it will simply be a matter of growing up and adults acting like adults, having the dignity that comes with being mature, being the example the children and other adults will respect. If everyone stays in their own little secure world, eventually, the state of families will diminish to the point of extinction. This, in turn, will affect the overall family we live in called society.

To the men, it's time we step up and assume our roles and responsibilities as parents, spouses, and leaders. For too long, we have left our women with the tasks of being our superwomen and wonder women to our children. If we're not in relationships with our children's mothers, it should not negate the fact that our children want to see us, and we still have a responsibility to acknowledge them. It doesn't take an explanation; it's just the right thing to do.

To the women, remember in life it's not how fast you run, but rather how far you get that will make the difference in the long run and the end. What you put out in this life, you will get back. Don't plant oranges and expect apples to grow. In other words, treat your kids special now, so if you're blessed to live long enough, they will be there for you when boyfriends, clubbing, and keeping up with the Joneses will not matter. Women, regardless of if you love or even like your children's fathers, be the adult and encourage a relationship between them rather than getting new boyfriends and expecting the children to look at them like their fathers because you all have accepted them as your boyfriends. No matter what you tell children about how no good their fathers are and what they don't do, as soon as the children get old enough, they are going to do everything and anything it takes to find their fathers. To them, it won't be about toys they didn't get; it will only be about acceptance. So, even if you have found someone else to take their space, just remember that they still can't take the children's fathers place.

To the grandparents, if you are still young, that doesn't mean you have to act like you never grew up. To those who are elderly, your grandchildren should be a sign to you that you have lived to see a full life. Knowing your life was extended to many others, should inspire you to embrace that.

To everyone, put God at the head of your family. Pray together to stay together. Let faith be your sunrises and prayers be your sunsets. May God bless you and be with you all in love, life, health, and wealth.

The Death of A Matriarch

ACKNOWLEDGMENTS

I want to acknowledge my sister, Mrs. Shelia Mack, for all your good works with Mom. The way you were there for her was a testimony that she was a good mother.

The way you took it upon yourself to do everything she needed done was a beautiful thing. To see how love can conform itself to overcome any obstacle was a powerful thing to witness.

The way you sacrificed your life for years to take care of Mom reached up to the highest heavens to God, who has always been with you.

Shelia, thank you for always being there for me. You are truly my guardian angel. Thank you for carrying me when the burden placed on me was too heavy for me to walk with.

Thank you, beyond words, for taking care of my boys. You never cease to amaze me with how you are forever doing God's work and will. I am eternally grateful to you for being the best aunt to the boys and the best sister and friend to me.

I love you, and I wish you the best in love, life, health, and wealth. The qualities and attributes you have are an extension of Mom that allows me to see her light still scintillating through you.

– Love you, Sis

www.ingramcontent.com/pod-product-compliance
Lightning Source LLC
Chambersburg PA
CBHW071622040426
42452CB00009B/1449